A Collection of Miscellany Poems and Letters, Comical and Serious. By Jo.Harvey

A

COLLECTION

O F

Miscellany POEMS

A N D

LETTERS,

COMICAL and SERIOUS.

❖❖❖❖❖❖❖❖❖❖❖❖❖❖❖❖❖❖❖❖❖❖❖❖❖❖

By JO. HARVEY.

❖❖❖❖❖❖❖❖❖❖❖❖❖❖❖❖❖❖❖❖❖❖❖❖❖❖

Edinburgh, Printed for the Author. 1726.

( )

The RIGHT HONOURABLE,

T H E

Counteſs of PANMUIR.

MADAM,

 Have not adventur'd to Addreſs the following Trifles to a Perſon of your Illuſtrious Character, they have only fled to your Generoſity for Protection. That Countenance you have formerly given to ſome of

a   'em,

'em, without knowing the Author, hath encourag'd their Approach, and made thofe you have not feen, run greedily under the Influences of that Goodnefs, their Fellows had fo bountifully tafted before.

HAD thofe loofe Effays carried in them any Merit of their own, the Author might have been vain enough perhaps to have prefumed on a Dedication; But he's fo extremely fenfible of the Meannefs of his Prefent, that a bare Acceptance is his utmoft Ambition. Nor, would he have pretended, even to that, had he not been Sollicitous to difcharge himfelf of that Duty and Gratitude he

fo

( )

fo juftly ow'd, and which you had fo extraordinarily oblig'd him to.

GENEROSITy, Madam, is a Virtue that can adorn the Soul of a Peafant; But when it appears in Perfons of more diftinguifh'd Charaƈters, it raifes them, as it were, above Mortality, and attraƈts a Regard that borders upon Adoration.

THIS is a Principle that reaches all the Conditions of Mankind, and exerts it felf in the honourable, as well as in the charitable Scenes of Life.

'TWERE endlefs to bring Inftances of this noble Quality, from *Greece* or *Rome*,

or,

or, indeed, from any facred or profane Hiftorian : Nor does your particular Knowledge in thefe Matters, need the Affiftance of fo poor an Informer.

GENEROSITY, Madam, gave your great Anceftor to this Nation. A noble Difdain to hear a brave Man reproach'd, even in an Enemy, occafion'd his Departure from his Native Country, and made him ours. But I pafs over this Circumftance for the prefent, in hopes to take it up on a more proper Occafion. Nor need I trace this Character thro' the fucceeding Branches of your Illuftrious Family; that were but a poor Repetition of what all the World knew before, and

put

( )

putting an Affront upon the beſt Pens of our Nation.

BU T now, Madam, your ſelf ſtands fairly in the Way, attended with Greatneſs, Goodneſs, Senſe, Generoſity, and all the charming Topics of Panegyric! Nor cou'd it well be imagin'd, that the Author of ſuch an Addreſs ſhould paſs over Particulars; eſpecially ſince, without Flattery, he can give ſolid Inſtances. Yet I think he declines the Scene, upon better Grounds than he cou'd have ventur'd the Deſcription.

IF telling the World, that the Subejℓ is above his Genius, and that, like ill Face-

Pain-

( )

Painters, he fhou'd come far fhort of the bright Original, won't ferve the Turn; If the Fear of doing Violence to the Modefty of fo illuftrious a Perfonage, won't excufe the Encomium; yet, I hope, 'twill be allow'd, that to put you in Mind of your own Endowments, is but a flender (not to fay fuperfluous) Compliment, and to tell, you are Good and Generous to thofe who are continually feeling it, were a Solœcifm in common Manners, and a Banter upon the Sincerity of their Acknowledgments.

THUS, Madam, have I declin'd a Task, which I knew my felf unable to fuftain, and have fat down, with the reft

of

of the World, happy in the Experience of that Goodnefs we know not how to exprefs.

IF the following Trifles find Acceptance, 'tis owing to this Principle I have been infifting on, a Principle fo peculiar to the Great : If they are rejeded, I fhall own 'tis no more than they deferve ; but fhall comfort my felf with the Confcioufnefs of a well-meant Offering, and that I have only fallen a Sacrifice to my own Gratitude. In the mean Time, I am with the profoundeft Regard,

Madam,

Your moft Obedient,
Moft Oblig'd, and
Devoted Servant,
JO. HARVEY.

THE

PREFACE.

THERE's a certain Anxiety attends an Author, when he appears in Public, that he cou'd not have imagin'd before; or, if he had, he wou'd readily have been twice advis'd ere he had ventur'd upon the World.

His Moments (like thofe of a Lover) are divided betwixt Hope and Defpair, and his

b whole

whole Time mere Suspense and Imagination.
'Tis diverting to see him rise upon the Appro-
bation of his learn'd Friends, and in a Moment
fall before the Breath of a Mechanic: To see
him elated upon the Commendation of a Lady of Sense, but sink again under the Criticism
of a Waiting-Maid.

'Twere endless to run through all the alter-
native Joys and Agonies of a poor Author.
And, to say the Truth, though that Species of
Mortals (of all others) is at most Pains to
please the World, the World is pretty often
very ungrateful in its Returns. Therefore it
is, that the poor Beings must have Recourse to
Prefaces, &c. in Order to clear themselves
of some real, but many more imaginary Impu-
tations. However, though I have as much Reason as any Man, to go into this Method of
Prefacing, yet I have thought fit to supersede
it at present, and to tell the Reader, that as

this

this is the firft Opportunity I have had, of ma-
king any public Acknowledgment of the Kind-
nefs formerly fhewn me-by my Friends, I cou'd
not, in Duty fail to embrace it with all the
grateful Refentment I was capable of. I know
them too well, not to own it was in their Pow-
er, to have treated my little Perfoimances a_s
they deferv'd : But that Influence which they
cou'd have eafily imploy'd againft me, they
have turn'd to my Advantage, and have laid
afide their own fuperiour Genius's, to favour
one who has no Pretenfions, but to their
Friendfhip.

There is one Fault indeed they are guilty of,
which I fhall ever iegrete, till I fee it redref-
fed ; and that is, their extreme, or, fhall I call
it, their vitious Modefty.

There is a Set of young Gentlemen amongft
us (to fome of whom I have the Honour to be
known)who are Mafters of as politeand elegant

a

a Stile, either in **Profe** or Numbers, as fome perhaps, even celebrated Writers elfewhere. But fuch an extraordinary Bafhfulnefs poffeffes them, that 'tis next to impoffible to prevail with them, to favour One with a Sight of any Production of theirs, if it is not a very particular, intimate **Friend.** This is a vicious Kind of Modefty indeed! and the Effects of it are very Pernicious: For if a Perfon of Birth and Education gets himfelf into fuch a Habit of Diffidence (and it will, like other Things, grow into a Habit) that he dares not expofe fo much as his Writings to the View of Mankind, tho' never fo confcious of his own Senfe and Merit; How fhall he exert himfelf in the Behalf of his Friend or his Countrey, or indeed, in any generous Concern, if Matters required his utmoft Affurance and Addrefs? This, I fay, is a Fault! and fuch an one, as the old *Greeks* and *Romans* wou'd have had rectified at any Expence. If it were re-
quir'd

quit'd of our Gentlemen, to fhow their Confi-
dence in a Campaign, they won't ftick at that,
I'll anfwer for't ; But there is as much Ufe
foi Courage and Addrefs in the Civil, as in the
Military Life ; Nor do we ever read of an
Athenian or a *Roman*, whofe early Appearances
in a learned or civil Capacity, don't ftand as
bright upon Record, as his greateft Actions in
the Field. The Author of a fhining Peiform-
ance in his Clofet, is as fecure of Fame, as the
Conqueror of Cities and Countreys ; Nor are
the Writers of the *Iliad* and *Æneid* lefs Immortal, than the Heroes they defcribe.

But perhaps there is one Way to account
for this deplorable Diftemper, and that is,
the byafs'd Tafte of fome, even grave and ju-
dicious People, of our Nation. They have
got a Tradition among them, which they
ftick too clofe to in all Confcience, and 'tis this,
If a Man writes out of the common Road, in
Profe

Profe or Numbers (but efpecially in Numbers)
Why, he's Airy or Pedantic, or Light i'th'
Head; which is all one as to fay, he's a Fool,
or a Madman. Now, 'tis certainly no Wonder,
if a Gentleman fhould be afraid to expofe the
politeft Performance, fince he's, in a Manner,
fure to meet with fuch a Character for his
Pains. And this, I think, may be one Reafon,
why our beft Productions of this Kind, ly
ftiffled and unknown. But will thofe grave
Gentlemen tell me, Were the *Greeks* and the
Romans all Fools and Madmen? No Body,
that I know of, has affirmed fo; and yet,
their feveral States have been manag'd by the
politeft Writers of their Times.

The Poets (a Name which perhaps we may
have the worft Notions of) *viz. Sophocles, Eu-*
ripides, Æfchylus, and many others among the
Greeks, were the Companions of their feveral
Law-

Law-givers, and their Writings have afforded them their very Maxims of State.

Among the *Romans,* every one knows how they were efteem'd ; They were the intimate Friends of the higheft Officers of State, the Confidents of the greateft Emperors, and had, generally fpeaking, the Key and Secret of the Empire. If a Poet now fhou'd fcruple to vifit his Prince upon Invitation, he wou'd be reck-on'd mad indeed: But this has happen'd, and that to a Prince fuperior to all thofe in *Eu-rope* put together, and yet no Offence taken.

A Poet had the Honour to be confulted, and to Determine that fame Prince in one of the niceft Points that ever concern'd the *Roman* Empire. Thus the Ancients reckon'd a Poet neither a Fool nor a Madman. And if we come down to the Moderns, let us obferve the *French* Nation ; A Nation, fince the Reign of *Charles* the Great, but obfcure, and little regarded; till by the Encouragement and

c. Ex-

Example of thofe noble and learned Minifters, the Cardinals *Richlieu* and *Mazarini*, and under the Influences of their late Sovereign *Lewis le Grand* (tho' no Scholar himfelf, but a Man of extraordinary natural Endowments) they rofe in Arts and Arms, to the Admiration, as well as Terror, of all *Europe*. And yet a Poet was the Perfon, whom that Prince honour'd with particular Orders to write his Life. And it was the Pride, as well as the Satisfaction of Cardinal *Richlieu*, to Share in the Performances of Mr. *Corneille*, which, the Refentment he fhow'd at his being excluded a part in one of them, puts beyond Difpute.

If we take a View of our Neighbours the *Englifh*, we fhall find that Art encourag'd and practis'd by the greateft among them, both in Church and State. As every other Branch of Learning fhines now with the higheft Luftre in that Nation, and, as at this Day they excel all the World in their Reputation, both for

Arts

A·ts and Arms, fo in this, they feem to excel themfelves, and to vye with the greateft Genius's of Antiquity. Their Bifhops, their Chancellois, their Treafurers, their Secretaries, Ambaffadois, and moft of their Officers Civil and Ecclefiaftic, have one Time or other adorned this Art; nor would fome of them quit the Reputation they have gained by it, for the Dignity of their other Titles or Preferments. And if we fhould call thefe People light-headed, or the Prince a Fool that employs them, I am afraid the late Treaty they managed with us, will be too ready to give us the Lie, and be a fad Witnefs againft us, how far our Wifdom and Gravity was out-done by their Levity and Poetry.

I might adduce feveral other Reafons, why the Study of polite Writing (unlefs by a few young Gentlemen) is fo little known or efteemed amongft us; and that which the *French* call the *Bon Goute*, is fo much neglected, or rather

ther

ther ridicul'd by our Nation: But I shall wave them at present; only this I must humbly offer, That if perhaps the Method of our Schools were alter'd, and set upon a Footing with those of *England* or *France*, we might come to make as handsom Appearances in any Part of the *Belles Lettres*, as they do; though at present we must own our selves obliged to these two Nations, for any Taste we have of the Ancients at all.

As to the following Trifles, all I shall say, is, That they were a Parcel of occasional Papers, written for the Diversion of some particular Friends; and (excepting one or two of them) never design'd for the Publick. However, since they have come Abroad, if the Reader can find any Entertainment by them; or, if they can induce those of higher Capacities, to oblige their Country with their Productions, I shall not think my Labour, or my Time, bestow'd in vain.

TO THE
MEMORY
O F
The Illustrious PRINCESS,

ANNE Dutchess of HAMILTON,

Who died at her Apartments in the Palace
of *Holy-rood-house*, *August* 1724.

GONE then, Illustrious Fair ! And shall the Muse
　　Her Duty to thy Memory refuse?
No, no, The Muse attends the sacred Hearse,
With the just Tribute of a native Verse
Trembling she stands, and views the dismal Scene,
And in sad Accents thus repeats the Strain ———
Gone then, illustrious Fair ! The Eccho's round,
In hollow Notes, return the dying Sound.

A　　　　　　　　With

With Thee all Virtues and all Goodnefs fly,
Abandon Earth, and haften to the Sky.
The mournful Nymph, and the dejected Swain,
Amaz d, forfake the inaufpicious Plain ,
The feather'd Songfters, thro' the gloomy Groves,
Renounce their Mufick, and difclaim their Loves ,
Honour fits brooding on th' abandon'd Shore,
And the departed Graces charm no more.

Cou'd thine Angelick Form, or glorious Race,
Have added to the Number of thy Days ,
Thy matchlefs Beauty, and thy Princely State,
Had ftrove for Conqueft, and difputed Fate.
Cou'd all the Virtues blended in thine Heart,
Have ftood the Shock, or ftopt the fatal Dart ,
Then had the Tyrant aim'd his Shafts in Vain,
And the fair Saint had triumph'd on the Plain.

Fond Thoughts '

Nor durft thofe Shafts that heav'nly Form affail,
Nor cou'd the Tyrant o'er the Saint prevail.
Angels beheld her with a loving Eye,
All form'd for Blifs, and fitted for the Sky.

At

At once they bow before th' Immortal Throne,
And point where earthly Graces match their own

Then fpoke th' Almighty '

Seraphs ! Refcue the Saint from Pain and Noife,
And plant her Soul amidft your richeft Joys.

The Pow'rs obey'd !

Then ftraight a mighty Squadron wings its Way,
And downward rides, triumphant on the Day.
The floating Hoft, thro' Fields of fluid Air,
Reflects new Glories on each brightned Sphere
Thofe Regions paft, the gay Immortal Crowd,
All flaming, o'er the regal Fabrick ftood.
Juft as the Fair in pious Raptures rofe,
And for her Theme the Bleft Meffiah chofe ,
Lo ! thro' the Dome bright *Raphael* foftly ftole,
And 'midft th' Ejaculation catch'd her Soul.
Back thro' the Air they wing their rapid Way,
And rife in louder Anthems on the Day.

Ceafe then, Illuftrious Prince ! Nor ask Relief
From this wild Rage, and Luxury of Grief.

Mourn

Mourn not the pious Fair, nor let thy Cry
Moleſt th' Harmonious Seraphs on their Way:
Grateful reſign what God had kindly given,
Nor once diſpute the Property of Heav'n.

Adieu, Great Patriot, thy Grief controul,
And let her dear Remembrance charm thy Soul.
May her ſoft Image in thy Boſom reſt,
And ſooth, but ne'er torment thy faithful Breaſt:
May her new Glories on her Conſort ſhine,
And all her Joys be, by Reflexion, thine.
Thus happy mayſt thou live, Illuſtrious Soul!
'Till, late, thy Spirit, mounting to the Pole,
Shall meet thy Spouſe amidſt the Realms of Day,
And melt a ſoft Eternity away.

T O

TO THE

Ingenious AUTHOR of the following POEM.

AS *none but* Scots, *in Battle,* e'er defy'd
The Roman *Arms, and check'd their growing Pride,*
So Scotish *Bards alone with equal Fame,*
In Roman *Lays, cou'd vye with Ancient* Rome ,
Equal they foar'd aloft, with boundless Flight,
And left th' Inferiour Nations out of Sight !

But while they triumph thus in Latin *Bays,*
The Englifh *Bards, in* Englifh, *claim the Praife ·*
Pope's *fprightly* Genius *ftrives to gain the Race,*
And follows Homer *with an equal Pace ;*
And matchlefs Add'fon, *in his fam'd* Campaign,
Like Virgil's *Hero makes his* Marlbro' *fhine.*

Our Scotish *Swains have follow'd thefe in vain,*
Sibboleth *ftill confefs'd the native Strain:*
But You, my Friend, have in your Poem fhown
What Add'fon's *felf, without a Blufh, might own.*

The

The Valiant KEITH *no less than* Marlbro' *shines,*
Above in Merit, equal in thy Lines

Go on, *my Friend, in manly Verse inspire*
Our Scotish *Youth with Ancient* Scotish *Fire;*
Paint Bruce's *Actions in their brillant Light,*
And all the Glories of th' *unequal Fight ,*
Here Douglas *follow'd, There the* English *run,*
And Seas of Saxon Gore *swell'd* Bannock-Burn.

Tho' Scotia's Sons, *o' late degen'rate grown,*
Tamely gave up their Sov'reign and their Crown,
Inglorious Wretches! who their Country sold,
And meanly barter'd Liberty for Gold;
Slaves to the proud insulting Saxon Race,
How will they look their Fathers in the Face,
When in th' Elysian *Shades? if e'er they reach that Place.*

Yet some there are who injur'd Albion's *Right*
Dare still assert, and for her Cause dare Fight ,
True Fergus' Sons, *of whose untainted Blood*
No sordid Drop e'er stain'd the Crimson Flood:
These be thy Theme, their glorious Acts proclaim,
And Eternize thy Numbers in their Fame

GEO. DENUNE, M.D.

TO THE
MEMORY
OF
The Right Honourable,

WILLIAM late Earl of KINTORE.

Hilst Thou, Great Soul, pursu'st Thy airy Way,
Mount'st on a Thought, and bear'st on endless Day,
Whilst, on Immortal Wing, Thou skim'st the Skies,
And view'st the whirling Orbs with vast Surprize ·
Now whilst, Sublime, Thou soar'st above the Pole,
Where Matter is no more, and no more Worlds roll .

Pleafe ftoop, Great Shade, a Moment on thy Wing,
And hear an humble Bard devoutly fing.

Fain

Fain wou d I all Thy ancient Glory trace,

And fing th' immortal Honours of Thy Race .

Confcious of native Weaknefs, all in vain,

An humble Mufe attempts the Lofty Strain.

Whilft I the vaft, the arducus Task purfue,

What Scenes of Wonder open to my View ?

Glories on Glories, ftill fuccefive, rife,

Whilft all th' immortal Race affert their native Skies !

Yet fondly ftill the Mufe attempts their Fame,

And ftill, unequal, finks beneath the arduous Theme

So fprightly *Pope* doth all his Force engage

To reach the Heig'ts of the *Mæonian* Page ,

Sublime on daring Wing, thro' Paths ne'er trod,

He views Great *Homer* tew'ring like a God ;

Fired with unequal Rage, he toils in vain,

And heaves, and gafps, oppreft beneath the mighty

    Scene.

Ye Pow'rs! Be kind for once, For once infpire

A willing Genius with uncommon Fire.

And Thou, Great Shade, dart, from thy native Skies,

A Smile propitious, on my feeble Lays.

I feel th' infpiring Ray ! ——— my Spirits rowl ;

                                    And

And Tides of Rapture ſwell my lab'ring Soul.
Where ſhall the Muſe thy Ancient Glories trace?
Back to fam'd *Barry* let us haſte apace.

Triumphant *Sweno*, inſolently proud,
In all the Pomp of Luſt and Rapine rode
Thro' ruin'd *England*, which oppos'd in vain,
And, conquer'd, tamely dragg'd th' inglorious Chain.
How did the bold ſucceſsful Tyrant ſmile,
Hoping to bound his Conqueſt with the Iſle ?
Againſt the *Scots* his conqu'ring Arms he bends,
And Hardy *Camus*, to reduce them, ſends.

From *Cimbrian* Shores, in haſte, the warlike *Dane*,
Thirſting for Glory, lanches to the Main.
Swift, with inſpiring Gales, he's wafted o'er,
And, in *Bodotria's* Channel, ſeeks the Shore.

Vain Enterprize ! ———

In ſhining Steel the *Scotiſh* Squadrons ſtand,
And Death and Terror guard the fatal Strand.
Enrag'd, he turns, and ſkimming *Roſſia's* Coaſts,
On Fair *Æneia's* Shore he lands the Barb'rous Hoſt:

B   No

No fooner from their Ships the Troops defcend,
Put Sword and Fire and Ruin wafte the Land
They all the Villages to Afhes turn,
And, with devouring Flames, the yellow Harvefts burn,
Alarm'd, Great Malcolm, ere it was too late,
Haftes to prevent his fink ng Country's Fate,
Straightway the Gilded Lyon waves in Air,
Round which, in Throngs, the daring Scots appear,
Their native Rights all eager to affert,
Glory and Freedom glows in ev'ry Heart
With Care paternal, anxious Malcolm fcanns
Th' Events of War, and conquer'd England's Chains.

Now did the rapid Sun his Beams difplay,
And, mounting, darts around the dreadful Day;
The Hoftile Squadrons now each other view'd,
Glitt'ring in horrid Iron, the Legions ftood
In terrible Aray, Extended far
O'er Barry's direful Plains, a dreadful Length of War!
Their fhining Arms reflect the blended Rays,
And flafh on either Hoft a difmal Blaze.
Thus rang'd in fteely Pomp, and deep Aray,
The eager Troops demand the bloody Day.

Then

Then ftreight the fprightly Trumpet, from afar,
Swelling with awful Clang, infpires the War :
And whilft the Hills the loud Alarm rebound,
Each Hero feels his Soul dilating with the Sound.

But, O my Mufe, what Numbers wilt thou find,
To fing the ancient *Scots* in Battle joyn'd ?
The Signal given , Wing'd with impetuous Rage,
The Rapid Squadrons furioufly engage !
So rufh the warring Elements on high,
When Tides meet Tides encount'ring in the Sky ;
When wat'ry Floods and Flames together roll,
And, with their hideous Roar, confound the Pole.

Now Hate and Glory fire their Souls by Turns,
And in full Fury all the Battle burns.
From temper'd Steel the ftreaming Flafhes fly,
Blending a horrid Gleam, and mingling with the Day!
The Rufhing Nations mix their difmal Cries,
And Shouts and dying Grones torment the Skies.

With former Succefs flufh'd th' infulting *Dane*,
Born on a rapid Courfer, fcours the Plain,

Urging

Urging the War ; The *Scotiſh* Troops give Way,
Confus'd in Heaps expiring Squadrons lay,
And anxious *Malcolm* ſees the ſad declining Day.
With ſudden Dread he feels his Spirits chill'd,
And Pale, and Hopeleſs, views the deadly Field.

Now, Gen'rous *KEITH*! Now does Thy awful Name
Commence its Glory in the Rolls of Fame
Hail, Godlike Youth! who, fir'd with gen'rous Grief,
Flew to Thy Country's, and Thy King's Relief,
Born on Revenge, Thou wing'ſt Thy dreadful Way,
Ruſhing thro' all the Havock of the Day ,
Thro' Death and Ruin driv'ſt upon Thy Foes,
Reſtor'ſt Thy Country's Honour, and the Cauſe
In Heaps expiring ly the mangled *Danes,*
And Hills of Carnage glut the fatal Plains.
The rapid *Lochty,* choak'd with Tides of Blood,
Rolls, groning, to the Sea, a Crimſon Flood.
Slaughter, with clotted Hair, and pale Diſmay,
Stalk ghaſtly o'er the Ruins of the Day.

Thus at fam'd *Loncarty,* when murd'ring *Danes*
Had drove the *Scotiſh* Legions from the Plains ;

Un-

Undaunted *H A T* beholds the shameful Foil,
And swiftly rushing from his homely Toil,
Choaks the base Flight, and bars the Victor's Way,
And, Thund'ring with his Yoke, restores the Day.

Illustrious *H A T !* O may thy ancient Name,
Thy Country's early Pride! The Muses Theme!
Ne'er be forgotten in the List of Fame.
Bright, as Thy self, may all Thy godlike Line
For ever in the *Scotish* Annals shine.

Thus then, Great *Keith,* from rescu'd *Scotland's* Fate
Thy Train of ancient Honours takes its Date.
Malcolm, who strictly cou'd the Field survey,
Soon had Thy great Ancestor in his Eye;
And those high Marks of Honour straight bestows,
That justly to his Services he owes,
Which, in their native Splendour, still unstain'd,
His Godlike Sons have gloriously maintain'd.

Fain wou'd I sing each Hero of the Line,
But the vast Task controuls the just Design;
For ne'er did Fortune raise or sink the State,
But each brave *KEITH* still shar'd his Country's Fate.

Muſt then, Illuſtrious Shade, th' ungrateful Muſe
Her Tribute to thy gen'rous Sire refuſe?
No, no; For ever may his Glory live,
Brightned with all the Charms the Muſe can give.
In *Scotland* ever be his Name obſerv'd,
Dear to her as the Honours he preſerv'd.

Long had the Tyrant *Cromwel* proudly Reign'd,
And, bold in Succeſs, Gods and Men diſdain'd,
With impious Joy had ſeen his Conqueſts ſwell,
On Witchcraft founded, and ſecur'd by Hell.
Long had with Artifice, and ſly Pretence,
Abus'd the Nation, and confounded Senſe
Britain of all her Rights is quite bereav'd,
And with the Sound of Liberty enſlav'd.
Her Provinces o'errun, her Cities ſpoil'd,
Her Sov'reign butcher'd, and his Heirs exil'd.
Wrapt in his Gyant-crimes, he braves the Skies,
And Heav'n and Earth and all, but Hell, defyes.
Now wants he nothing to complete his Game,
But th' Enſigns Royal, and a Monarch's Name.
His too obſequious Friends miſtake the Plot,
Balk him in This, as did thy Sire in That.

Hail,

Hail, wondrous Youth! Who, obstinately Good,
Unmov'd, 'midst all the Shocks of Faction stood;
Consummate Prudence in thy Youth appears,
And Manly Wisdom decks thy Childish Years.
Early, in Thee, Nature her self outran,
And form'd the Patriot before the Man. ————

But now, Great Soul, Thy self, the Muse's Theme,
Her Energy commands, and all her Flame.
She views thee shining in thy double Charms,
Renown'd in Piety, as well's in Arms.
The Hero and the Saint divide her Lays,
Both she admires, and knows not where to praise.
If trac'd to thy Retirement, we shall find
Thy Moments all Devotion, all resign'd.
When Hearts like thine feel Heav'n's inspiring Rays,
They shed around no faint, no vulgar Blaze.
Uncommon Raptures thro' the Vitals roll,
And Flames of Ardour bear the mounting Soul.
Thus oft, by Pray'r, thy Mind all rais'd on High,
Was lost in Bliss, and liv'd on Extasy.
Nor stood thy Piety in this alone,

The Theory bright in the Practice shone,
Thy lib'ral Hand still dealt thy bounteous Store,
Reliev'd the Needy, and supply'd the Poor

But hark! Once more *Bellona* sounds to Arms,
And daring *Scots* are ravisht with her Charms;
Undaunted to the Field they rush in Throngs,
All eager to redress their Country's Wrongs
Behold the Hero, with his warlike Train,
In martial Pomp, advancing to the Plain,
Unmov'd, He hears the Thund'ring Engines roar,
And, fearless, marches on thro' Tides of Gore.
Inspir'd with Rage, and with his Country's Cause,
He rushes, like a Torrent, on his Foes.
Confus'd around ly scatter'd Heaps of slain,
And Crimson Streams float o'er the Purple Plain.

But ah! Great *George*, how shall my Thoughts get free
To speak the Fullness of my Soul for Thee?
We saw Thee, when, impatient of the Rein,
Thy bounding Courser paw'd the dusty Plain;
We saw Thee rush, (and wondred at the Sight!)
Dauntless thro' all the Ruins of the Fight;

When

When Thy vaft Soul, too prodigally Great,   (Fate!
Brav'd fulph'rous Storms, and Tempefts wing'd with
Immortal *George !*   we faw what Heaps of Foes
Fell Victims to thy Fury, and the Caufe. ———
But here the fetter'd Mufe muft skim the Shore,
Fain wou'd fhe rife, but knows fhe dares not foar.

Farewell, Great Shade!   But fee th' Illuftrious Fair
Melting in Woe, and plung'd in deep Defpair,
In all her Pomp of folemn Grief appears,
Beauteous in Clouds, and Charming in her Tears!
Ah! ceafe, Divinely Fair, thy ufelefs Cries,
And on thy blooming Off-fpring turn thine Eyes.
Reprefs each rifing Sigh, each pious Groan,
And view the Sire reviving in the Son:
The Son! whom ev'ry Grace confpires t' adorn,
To better Times, we hope, and fofter Periods born.

  Farewell, Great Shade! too long, with pious Strains
Th' officious Mufe thy facred Ear detains;
Too long fhe fondly dwells upon thy Praife,
In artlefs Numbers, and unmeafur'd Lays.
  —

                  Fare-

Farewell, Illuftrious Shade! purfue thy Way,
To the bright Regions of Eternal Day.
And whilft, on rapid Wing, thou bend'ft thy Flight
Thro' flaming Spheres, and Tides of Purple Light,
Where thou behold ft Omnipotence on High,
Enthron'd in Splendours, and a Blaze of Day!
There, while thou roam'ft in boundlefs Happinefs,
Loft in eternal Extafies of Blifs,
Here fhalt thou live Immortal in thy Fame,
And lateft Ages fhall applaud thy Name.

T

T O

The much Honoured,

ALEXANDER CAMPBELL,

Commiſſary of the Caſtle of *Edinburgh.*

WELL gen'rous Highland-man! We ſaw thy Strains,
Soft as the Breezes on *Evonian* Plains :
Like as the Stream that ſlakes the Weſtern Roe,
We ſaw thy pure untainted Numbers flow.
Proud to behold Thee 'midſt the Poet-Throng,
The tuneful Nine came crouding to the Song ;
Phœbus himſelf rejoyc'd to ſee the Swain
Advance Superiour, to adorn the Plain.

Soft

Soft were the Sounds, when *Campbell* touch'd the Lyre,
And deep th' Attention of the liftning Quire.
Each charming Cadence of the num'rous Song
Dy'd in th' Applaufes of the wond'ring Throng.

Hail, Godlike Man! Whom tuneful Bards of old,
And all the *Druids* from their Cells foretold.
Bards! Who at firft on Thine own Mountains Sung,
When Weftern Groves with runic Numbers rung.
Proud of their Son! Their airy Forms advance,
And, pois'd on Atoms, to thy Meafures dance.
Joyful they fee, what they had erft divin'd,
True ancient Strength, with modern Softnefs joyn'd.
Joyful they fee Thy bold infpiring Lays
At once tranfcend our Envy and our Praife:

But tell me how Thou cam'ft, Illuftrious Swain!
I' obferve a lonely Shepherd on the Plain?
The laft and meaneft of the tuneful Throng,
Poor as his Thoughts, and Artlefs as his Song,
Obfcurely born, where chilling Tempefts fly,
And Storms, inceffant, fweep a Northern Sky;

In

In Climes, where Hyperborean Billows roar,
And beat a Bleak inhofpitable Shore. ———

'Twas kind thus to regard a lowly Name,
Loft to all Merit, and unknown to Fame ;
'Twas kinder ftill, to Mark him in the Throng,
To own his Numbers, and approve his Song.

Hail, Gen'rous Man ! Still may Thy ancient Race,
The Camp, the Court, and Plain, unrival'd, Grace.
Behold thy Chief adorn'd with glorious Scars,
And deckt with Laurels brought from foreign Wars.
Blaregnies ftill refounds the Hero's Fame,
Reveres at once, and trembles at the Name.
Now fair *Augufta's* Court the Warriour Charms,
And *Ilay* fhines in Arts, as he in Arms.

A Gen'rous *Campbell* gives *Edina* Laws,
Supports the Weak, Afferts the injur'd Caufe;
Beneath his Influence, the Poor opprefs'd
Smiles in his Wrongs, fecure to be redrefs'd.
Fix'd to the Right, amidft our Jarrs unmov'd,
He's fear'd by all, by all efteem'd and lov'd.

Fare-

Farewell now, Gen'rous Swain, and pray Excufe
Thefe fainter Sallies of a bafhful Mufe;
So may thy Race ftill rife to Arts and Arms,
And Thou poffefs the fair *Campbella's* Charms.
Campbella ! late, the Boaft of ev'ry Grove,
Retires now, happy in her Virgin-Love;
Bleft in her faithful Swain, fhe quits the Shades,
And leaves to other Nymphs the lonely Glades.
Her blooming Progeny her Thoughts engage,
Advancing ftill in Beauty as in Age
Still may they bloom, and, like their Parents, reign,
The future Pride and Glory of the Plain.

To Mr. *L----*

SIR,

I Don't doubt you have obferv'd our Idea's of Mankind, to rife and fall in Proportion to the Great-
nefs or Meannefs of the Places where they live, or
where they have been : The Houfe of a Farmer
raifes our Notions of him above what we conceive
of a Cottager ; as that of the Landlord exalts him a-
bove the Farmer. When I was in the North-Coun-
try, I knew a very infignificant Fellow, but that he
liv'd in *Aberdeen* ; and another inexplicable Blockhead, that rofe upon us, by being a Tradefman in
Edinburgh. I have feen a trigg Fellow of a Taylor
here, ecclips'd by a Broker at *London* ; and a Knot
of our Trone-men, offer all manner of Refpect to a
Porter of that Metropolis. I have known a very
good

good Mufician, but that he never was in *Italy*; and a very handfom Dancer, had he been able to make the Tour of *Paris* 'Tis extremely unaccountable, that a Fellow muft no fooner come from a neighbour-ing City or Country, but we fhall run in to all the Regard for what he fays, as if he had ,been fent to confult an Oracle, and had juft return'd with the Refponfes : That we fhould think fo meanly of our own Senfe, as to ftare at a Fool from *London* or *Paris*, like a Set of *Molucca* Savages, or a Nation of *Hottentots !* Nor are the Coxcombs unacquainted with this Method of Impofture· They know very well what Efteem a Twelve-month's Abfence from their Country procures 'em. And I have known a Quack, who could hardly breathe a Vein, actually tell me, he would go over to *Holland* for 6 or 7 Weeks, and then his Character, as a Phyfician, would be indif-putable. Is not this a pretty barefac'd Piece of Ban-ter upon the Senfe of his Countreymen? Muft he, becaufe he has feen *Leyden*, without knowing per-haps, or having been known to, any one Man of Senfe in it; affume over us as much, if not more than *Boerhaave* himfelf? Well, but thus it is;

and

and one that can tell better than you or I, whereabouts the *Scots* Dyke at *Rotterdam* lyes, is a Man of very fuperiour Learning, heighten'd with an extraordinary Exactnefs of Obfervation. Nay, let you or I but be defeat in the Geography of the Pier at *Amfterdam*, or the Pofition of a Crane at the *Briell*, we never can hold up our Heads in his Company, till we fhall have been upon the Spot, or come Home perhaps, and foil him in the Breadth of a Canal. 'Tis an odd Bus'nefs, that People won't learn to diftinguifh betwixt the Head and the Feet of a Traveller : This, one would think, were an eafy Matter, and yet very few will give themfelves that Trouble. I fay, few ; for fome Gentlemen there are among us, who, from the Advantages of a well grounded Education at Home, improv'd by a noble Tafte of Men and things Abroad, have return'd to their Country (after having done it fufficient Honour among thofe they have convers'd with) adorn'd with all the Qualities that are the Delight and Emulation of every Perfon of Judgment and Genius. So that, upon the Whole, it is not the Place where a Perfon lives, or the Countries he has feen, but a modeft and agreeable

Man-

Manner, joyn'd to a thorow and exact Education, that ought to pretend to our Affections, or gain upon our Regard. I am,

Sir,

Yours, &c.

To Mr. *B*----

S I R,

I Have fall'n through my Philofophy too much, to pretend to any further Skill in reafoning now, befides what mere natural Thinking, and what we call common Experience, prefents to me. Mr. *L*-- (and I hope you won't grudge that Advantage to one who is fo fond to fee any thing from you) has been fo kind as let me fee one of your Letters: You are pleas'd to fay there, and I'm as fond to believe what you fay, That there are Three things neceffarily in-
cluded

cluded in Senſation, *viz.* 1. The Cauſe, 2 The Mean or *Medium.* 3. The Effect, or the Idea. The laſt of theſe, you ſay, is only in our Minds. Now I ſhall ſuppoſe this Table, on which I am writing, is the Object of my Senſation at preſent The firſt thing I perceive in it, or, if you will, that it affects my Senſes with, is its oval Figure, its browniſh Colour, its being hard in a comparative Degree, *&c.* Now, I ſhould be very fond to think with you, that all theſe Things, Qualities, or Accidents, or what you'll pleaſe to call 'em, had a Self-Subſiſtence, or inher'd, at leaſt, in a Subject diſtinct from, and independent of, the Mind of any Perceiver. But, as the Qualities, Oval, Brown, Hard, *&c.* are certainly mere Creatures of the Imagination; ſo this Spark at *Dublin, Barclay,* won't allow me to think I have any thing elſe in my Table but theſe. He bids me ſee if I can find out any more than theſe Qualities, or if I can find out any Subſtance or *Subſtratum* diſtinct from them. I thought on it, and after I had divided a Bit of it in a thouſand Million of Atoms, I'll ſwear I could find no more than I have told you, *viz.* Colour, Extenſion, Hardneſs, *&c.* mere Notions I'gad! Upon this, Sir, I thought fit to

ſtep

ſtep down to *John* C—g (that was the Man that made
it) and ask'd him, How the Devil he cou'd put ſuch a
whimſical Table upon me, I did not expect it of him,
and all that? The honeſt Man ſeem'd ſurpriz'd, and
ask'd me what I meant, or if I was well enough?
Well enough, ſays I! I'm ſufficiently well, but I did
not look for this at your Hands. Lord! What's the
Matter, ſays he? The Matter, Man! Gadzooks, you
have given me a Table without any Subſtance in it
at all. As I'm a Sinner, Man, quoth he, I have given
you as ſubſtantial a Wainſcot Table, as ever I made in
my Life. Where then is that Subſtance, ſaid I? Is it
above, or below, or in the Middle of it? Pray let me
know, you that underſtand Timber-work, for I am
told, I have nothing but mere Whim and Fancy, and
you have trick'd me out of my Money, and given me
nothing but what I had of my own before I employ'd
you. This is the damn'dſt Maggot, ſays *John*. I vow,
I am cheated confoundedly, for, I have a vaſt Quantity of Notions in my Shop, and how to diſpoſe of 'em
the Devil knows I'm ſorry for it, *John*, ſays I, but
where came you by them? I, as I ſhall anſwer, I
bought them at *Leith*, and gave half a Crown for every

Idea

Idea of them. Say you fo, Faith 'tis a Hardfhip. Hardfhip! Rot him! They fay 'tis fome *Irifh* Bugar has put
thefe damn'd Fancies in Peoples Heads, to tell me my
Timber's Notions! By *Jove*, my Timber's as good
Timber as one could wifh to lay an Ax on. There's
no Help for it, *John* · Fare you well.   Farewel Sir,
but confound that *Irifh* Son of a ----, if ever our Cor-
poration gets hold of him ----- I wonder if the Smiths
have got Notice of this Affair yet? No, but there's a
horrid Noife among the Webfters, fome body has told
them, they're weaving mere Notions, and Webs of
Air. There's a curs'd Clutter yonder.

Dear Sir, I had not given you the Trouble of all
this, if the Learn'd did not think there were fome-
thing in it, and that amidft your fine Demonftration
of the Exiftence of Matter, you'll find, you're demon-
ftrating your own Idea's; and inftead of dividing your
Inch-Line into 10000 Parts, you may come to find, you
are dividing an Inch-Idea into 10000 Notions. I am,

Sir,

Yours, &c.

To

To the Ingenious Author of the following POEM.

NO, *happy Man! The Bays shall not be thine;*
 I'll pluck 'em from thy Brows, to place on mine.
How cou'd you think I e'er wou'd quit the Field,
And undisputed Laurels tamely yield?
What tho' with Ease and Strength your Numbers flow?
In mine, sure, equal Ease and Strength I'll show.
But ah! in yours a heav'nly Train appear!
Awful their Beauties, and their Charms severe!
With Love and Reverence they strike mine Eyes,
And force me, spite o' me, to yield the Prize.
To sing of such a Heav'n, with such Success!
A Pope, *or* Tickel *had expected less.*
But stay, with the same Breath I praise and blame,
With you an equal Share of Bays I claim;
Tho' you deserve a greater Share than them.
When Envy blinds us, when misled by Pride,
Reason must yield, and Judgment cease to guide:

So if a Charioteer fhould drop the Rein,
Th' unruly Courfers, whom no Bit reftrain,
Scour o'er the Fields, the Coach in Pieces flies;
Here ly the Wheels, and there the Coachman lies.

I yield, I yield! I own my felf o'ercome;
The Beauties of your Verfe have ftruck me dumb.
I'm humbly pleas'd to be the Mufes Friend,
Tou to a nobler Title now pretend;
The bright Affembly's Poet' that's a Name
To which Apollo proudly might lay Claim.

To the Illuſtrious

Aſſembly of Ladies at E D I N B U R G H,

A

P O E M

Humbly inſcrib'd, To the Right Honourable

The Ladies D I R E C T R E S S E S.

Qualis in Eurotæ ripis, aut per juga Cynthi
Exercet Diana choros; quam mille ſecutæ
Hinc atque hinc glomerantur OREADES——

                   VIRG.

SHALL Heav'n o'er *Albion* ſhed ſo kind a Ray,
    And not one Bard ſalute the blisful Day ?
Muſes attend ! Our zealous Rancour ſcorn,
And hail, in ſofteſt Notes, the joyful Morn!

                        See !

See! how the Dawn teems with a beauteous Train
Of Angel-Forms, defcending on the Plain.
In Sylvan Shapes the Nymphs divine appear,
Out-bloom the Spring, and brighten all the Year.

Their facred Souls Celeftial Vertue arms;
Awful their Beauties, and fevere their Charms!
By Heav'n commiffion'd to inftruct our Dames,
Direct their Thoughts, and regulate their Flames;
To guide the unexperienc'd Virgin o'er
Thofe Shelves o' Life their Virtue fhun'd before;
To calm our Heats, allay feditious Jars,
And finifh all our dire religious Wars.

Hail, happy Day! For ever white appear,
Great Feftival, and Glory of our Year!
Thrice happy Day! in which kind Heav'n takes Care
T' unite all Principles amongft the Fair!
No more fhall *Whig* and *Tory* kindle Wars,
Diftract our Morals, and divide our Pray'rs,
Names here on Earth to diff'rent Int'refts giv'n,
But all our Int'refts are the fame in Heav'n.

Hail,

Hail, Goddeſſes ! Behold th' attending Train
Of Nymphs and Swains that grace th' enamel'd Plain:
In various Paſtimes roam amidſt the Shades,
Sport on the Lawns, or trip alongſt the Glades.
Each Goddeſs here her heav'nly Gifts imparts,
And fills with gen'rous Thoughts their Virgin-hearts.
Amidſt Ambroſial Repaſts, in the Groves,
Refines their Taſtes, and all their Souls improves :
Or where the Choirs on yonder Plains advance,
And in bright Meaſures grace the num'ious Dance ;
A guardian Goddeſs ſtill attends the Fair,
Corrects their Motions, and improves their Air,
With conſcious Worth their Virgin-boſoms warms,
Exalts each Grace, and doubles all their Charms !

Go on, kind Guardian-Powers, let *Albion*'s Fair
Your Thoughts employ, and be your heav'nly Care.
As the bright Stars, in ſhining Rounds above,
Guided by their Intelligences, move,
Inform'd by Angel-Pow rs, unerring roll
Round the vaſt Circle of the azure Pole :

Guided

Guided by you, fo fhall our Stars below,

(That with more bright, more heav'nly Radiance
    glow)

The fhining Rounds of Virtue nobly run,

And greatly finifh what you have begun,

By you inform'd, fhall grace each Scene of Life,

The lovely Virgin, and more lovely Wife.

Till late, with yours, their Souls fhall upward fly,

The Earth abandon, to adorn the Sky.

Vir0

Viro Maximopere, fufpiciendo

Domino *Joanni Lauder*

a *Fountainhall*, Eq; Aurato,

Summæ, apud *Caledonios*, Forenfis Curiæ Sen.
Digniff.

Jo. Harvæus, uti par eft, *Salutem.*

Ergone mufa filet, carpit dum oblivia vitæ
    Sollicitæ, noftri gloria prima fo i?
Tot decoraffe finet roftra, aut fubfellia luftris
    Carmine inornatum fævus Apollo virum?
Mufa ades, & leges noftras, noftra affere jura;
    Pangito & Aonio carmina digna Deo:

Carmina

Carmina pange viro ' decorant que in dogmata legum,
   Juraque * per cives æqua tributa suos.

Ut stupuere sui quondam Demosthenis ora
   Cecropidæ, Hyblæis mistaque verba favis;

Utque olim ingentes animos, Romanaque corda
   Tullius eloquii flexerat arte sui,

Sic stupuit, *Laudere*, tuæ miracula linguæ,
   Cuncta *Caledonii* turba diserta fori.

Musa canat Graios, sanctumve Solona, Lycurgum,
   Seu canat, Ausonius Pompiliumve Modis;

Sive Asopiaden, seu Gnossia numina dicat;
   Cunctos *Lauderi* nomine musa canit.

Ut Patriis atavus quondam *Lauderus* in oris
   Asseruit forti *Scoticæ* jura manu;

Ut cinctum tremuere virum fulgentibus armis
   Saxonidum variis agmina fusa locis;

Sic vestræ insontes texit facundia linguæ,
   Sic tremuit leges impia turba tuas.

Quid

---

* *Victorque Volentes*

Per Populos dat Jura, viamque adfectat Olympo. Virg.
   Georg. 4. *sub finem*.

Quid referam aut mores fanctos, cognatave Cœlo

Pectora quid referam ' Nam nifi nota feram.

Si canat aut rabiem *Batavi*, fi facta cruenta

    Mufa, Thyeftæa vix fuperanda dape ;

Et *Glencoanas* avidum te ulcifcier umbras

    (Pofthabitis Titulis) fi canat, æqua canit.

O quali Memorem, Judex fanctiffime, mufa

    Te Decus Aftræ, te Themidifque decus ;

Sola, Aftræa, jacent tua nunc altaria ; nemo

    Nunc tua fana colit, Nunc, Themi, Nemo tua.

Sed mea Mufa file, fallentis & otia vitæ

    Define carpentem Sollicitare virum.

T O

The MEMORY of

The Right Honourable,

The late Lady *Blantyre* :

A PASTORAL.

CHLOE and *LEONORA.*

CHLOE.

F LY, *Leonora*, Fly the fatal Scene,
  Here brooding Woes and Horrours damp the Plain :
The Spring no more the feather'd Warblers cheer,
But boding Owls and Ravens blaft the Year.

LEO-

LEONORA.

Whither, dear *Chloe*, are the Graces fled,
The Nymphs and Swains, that late adorn'd the Mead?
What means this awful Silence o'er the Groves?
Once the soft Seats, and Scenes of chastest Loves!

CHLOE.

Ceafe, *Leonora*, to renew my Smart,
To wound afresh this sad, this bleeding Heart;
Back to my Soul, fee! my chill'd Spirits throng,
And fault'ring Accents tremble on my Tongue.

LEONORA

Nay, deareft *Chloe*, grant my fond Requeft,
And pour thy Woes into my faithful Breast;
For thee my Share of Sorrows I'll fuftain,
And learn, tho' unacquainted, to complain.

CHLOE.

No *Leonora*, no; I'll weep alone,
I'll mourn for ever, my *Lucinda* gone!

Lucinda ! Glory of the *Sylvan* Reign,
Now pale and breathlefs ftretch'd upon the Plain.

LEONORA.

Lucinda dead! Ye Gods' —— or did I dream?
Or did I hear my dear *Lucinda*'s Name?
Lucinda dead! --- For ever flow my Tears,
Till my thin Form diffolve to follow her's.

CHLOE.

Yes, *Leonora*, we'll indulge our Woes,
And only in our Tears we'll find Repofe;
Live on our Sorrows, and ask no Relief,
But from the Rage and Luxury of Grief.

LEONORA.

But fee! young *Strephon*, in yon lonely Grove,
Diffolves in Sighs, for his departed Love,
What Floods of Tears his youthful Face diftain!
Once the Delight, and Wonder of the Plain.

F   CHLOE.

CHLOE.

Ah, *Leanora*, ah ! the difmal Day !
When in the Gafps of Death *Lucinda* lay ;
How to his Lips he prefs'd th' expiring Fair,
To catch the Soul as it diffolv'd in Air.

LEONORA

Tell me, my *Chloe*, by our Friendfhip, tell
Our dear *Lucinda*'s dying laft Farewell ;
How fhe to *Strephon* fpoke that laft 'Adieu,
And what her dying Lips pronounc'd to you.

CHLOE

Yes, *Leonora*, I'll unfold that Scene,
'Twill roufe my Woes, and wake my languid Pain ,
I'll tell Thee —Firft when Death approach'd her Soul,
And I beheld her fwimming Eye-balls rowl ,
All bath'd in Tears, and plung'd in deep Defpair,
Straight to a Cyprefs Grove I bore the Fair ;
While Nymphs around, and Swains, with piteous Cries,
Fill all the Woods, and rend the echoing Skies'
Th' expiring Fair caft her dim Eyes around,

And

And fees their falling Tears bedew the Ground,

Adieu, ye Nymphs, fhe faid —— adieu ye Swains,

And all the foft Illufion of the Plains!

Adieu, my deareft *Chloe*, and to you,

My dearer *Strephon*, a long, long Adieu!

This *Strephon* heard, and furious with Defpair,

Forward he rufh'd, and clafp'd th' expiring Fair;

O Gods, he cry'd, Relentlefs and Unkind!

Is my *Lucinda* gone, and *Strephon* left behind?

No, no, *Lucinda*! we fhall never part,

Our Spirit fhall be one, as is our Heart;

Strephon fhall grow for ever to thy Breaft,

'Till Death unites us in eternal Reft.

At *Strephon*'s Name once more fhe rais'd her Eyes,

And whifpering, Farewell my *Strephon* — Dies.

LEONORA.

Ah *Chloe*! drop that difmal Scene of Death,

Or 'midft my Tears I muft refign my Breath;

Round my fad Heart a deadly Horrour reigns,

And my chill'd Blood ftands curdl'd in my Veins.

CHLOE.

CHLOE.

Then *Leonora*, I beheld the Fair
Spring upward thro' the Fields of fluid Air ,
Quick I beheld the Dove-like Form arife,
As from the Fun'ral Pile, and reach the Skies.
I faw an Argel-Train, in bright Aray,
On Azure Wings defcending thro' the Day;
The fpotlefs Spirit on her Way they meet,
And the fair Form with heav'nly Anthems Greet ,
At laft, thro' brighter Fields of Purple Light,
They foar'd, Triumphant, from my Mortal Sight.

T O

To Mr. S——

SIR,

THese are to let you know, that I am in good Health, bleſſed be God for it, wiſhing to hear the like from you. Your Uncle *John* ſits ay ſtill in the Mill-Tack. But is na our *Tibbie* faln wi' Bairn to the Miniſter's Man, and *Eppie* is marrried to *Geordie Strang*, gif ſhe's brown a guid Browſt ſhe'll drink the better o't. 'Tis a very cold Day this, I'll defend Nonſenſe againſt any Man for half an Hour. We hear the *Turk* has beat the *Czar* curs'dly at *Affracan*. The Meal's at Eight and a Babee the Peck *Num ens formale vel ens materiale ſit objectum metaphyſica* is a great Queſtion I hope your bliſtring Plaiſter has done very well, &c.

Pray, my Dear, let me know whether you have a Tranſlation of *Tacitus*. I am,

Yours &c.

TO

To Mr. *L----*

SIR,

WHen we have trac'd the Series of Generation backwards, thro' all the Steps of Addition, we muſt conclude the World to have been ſtill as full of Animals, as it is now, or, otherwiſe, we muſt ſtop at ſome one, and own a Creation. The *Dilemma* will prove equally hard in both Caſes For, if we ſay the Creatures were as numerous always as now, the Queſtion will be, How came they there? Either they produc'd themſelves, or not · If not, we muſt own a Creation from another Hand; if they did, then they exiſted before they were produced. I hope there is a ſufficient Enumeration (as the Logicians call it) in this *Dilemma*; nor can I imagine any third Way. But

if

if we fhou'd ftop (as faid is) at fome particular one, then the Queftion will be the fame again, *viz.* How came that Fellow there? And the Reafoning, as above. I love Brevity, and fhall conclude with,

Sir,

Your individual humble Servant,

Jo. Enthymeme.

To Mr. C---

SIR,

HAving got a little Time, and Sicknefs upon my Hands, I refolve to dedicate an Hour or two of it to you.

When one is confin'd at home, to the little fond Tattle of a Wife, and the inarticulate Pleafantries of a Wee-ane, (pleafe pardon the *Scots* of the Expreffion) he muft forget himfelf a little, in order to his prefent Entertainment, and lay himfelf afide a while, that he may enjoy himfelf the better.

1 don't know, if I make my felf underftood But, if I have not hitherto, I fhall proceed to the Explanation:

My Wife and I happen'd, this Evening, to enter upon a certain Topic (only now and then were interrup-

ted

ted by a particular Gefture or Smile from the Wee-
ane, which fhe could never let pafs unobferved) I fay,
we entred upon a Topic, which, I muft own, I was
not much feen in , I mean, the Ufefulnefs and agreeable Behaviour of *Sheep* *Virgil* has not, throughout
his Paftorals, beftowed handfomer Characters on that
Species, than fhe defign'd them , only, that I be-
hoved to make fome Allowances, for the Difference
of Expreffion, betwixt that Poet and my Wife.

In fhort, fhe made *Sheep* almoft the Hinge of human Life, and had very near run Mankind out of
Exiftence without them I was aftonifh'd to fee her
raife the Argument fo high of a fudden, and knew
not in the World, how to bring her Idea's down with-
in human Ken, or reduce her to any Sort of Form or
Figure. At laft, I happen'd on a Medium, which
ftartled her a little, telling her, That, notwithftanding
the extraordinary Qualities, and the extreme foft and
quiet Deportment of that Creature, fhe had reafon'd
and declaim'd fo high upon; I fay, notwithftanding
all this, I told her, I knew a *Sheep*, (whom we commonly call a *Tupp)* give his Mafter a Blow on the

G   Hips,

Hips, as he was mending a Plough, which carry'd him quite over the faid Plough, into the moft ftinking Pond I had ever feen in my Life, upon which, his Mafter, being enrag'd, came with a Club to beat him. But while he was deliberating, betwixt ftriking him on a right Place, and one that might be dangerous, the Tupp fet him on his Hips a fecond Time, and then he leugh Upon which, fhe immediately askt, If the Tupp leugh? I was furpriz'd at that Queftion, and believ'd fhe was going to add that Circumftance to the reft of the Qualities of that Animal But reflecting, that I had left the true Nominative to my Verb *Leugh*, at a little too great Diftance, I brought it up and fhe found, at laft, it was the Tupp's Mafter that leugh.

In Obitum
PIÆ AC GENEROSISSIMÆ DOMINÆ,
D. a FOUNTAINHALL,
ELEGIDIUM,

April 18. 1713.

AN quia matrona es, generofo ftemmate nata,
 Fatorum rigido numine, fancta, cadis?
An quia conjugio generofo juncta marito,
Exofam Eumenides fortem habuere tuam?
An quia te fuperi generofa ftirpe bearant,
Hanc Atropos viduat fæva parente fua?
Haudquaquam, innocuam fpectans fine crimine vitam,
Nos tali indignos oibat at ipfe D E U S.

Si

Si pietas, morum candor, si lucida virtus,
Diftulerint vitæ fata dolenda tuæ;
Nec tua vel Parcis licuiffet rumpere fila.
Tam cito, fupremam vel properaffe diem.
At cunctis lugenda jaces, generofa propinquis,
Flebilis & juftis omnibus, atque piis.
Te dolet abreptam genitor, longævaqve mater,
Atque fua incaffum fletibus ore rigant
Incaffum tua fata dolent, fua damnaque plorant
Dulcis conjugii pignora chara tui.
Te tamen ante omnes, charus, viduufque maritus
Luget, & incaffum cuncta dolore replet.
Quid juvat immenfo præcordia rumpere motu,
Atque piæ lachrymæ quid, generofe, juvant?
Quid juvat affiduis ruptus plangoribus æther,
Quidve juvant mœftis tecta repleta fonis?
Poffe putas fuperos flecti vel fata precando?
Haudquaquam; exanimis, nec revocanda, jacet.
Comprecor idcirco triftes te ponere luctus,
Quum nullo confors fit reparanda modo,
Nam fua cuique dies ftat, & irrevocabile tempus,
Et brevis eft vitæ terminus ufque fua.

To

To Mr. *L*---- .

SIR,

'TIS the ftrangeft Thing in the World to find a Man without fome Whim or another, that predominates over all his other Affections and Inclinations; fome notional, airy Biafs, that overbalances his Reafon, and fuperfedes his calmeft Difcretion. I went t'other Night to vifit a poor Man in Prifon, and as there are a great many confin'd in that Place, I found amongft the reft a Gentleman of no contemptible Senfe, but fo extremely gone in the Politicks, that his Confinement, his Indigence, and Diftrefs, was a mere Jeft to a Paragraph in the *Caledonian Mercury.* I happen'd to drink a Glafs with him, together with fome others who had come in upon the fame charitable

defign,

defign, and he was going on to tell us his Story, and his Treatment by thofe who had incarcerate him, in a Manner that had certainly mov'd us to fpend another Peny upon his account ; but that fome of the Company unluckily askt me, What News ? He took up the Queftion with an amazing Violence, Nay, Gentlemen, fays he, you have not had fuch a Poft of a very long Time. A certain Friend interrupting him, Good Lord, Man, fays he, cannot you hear a Body fpeak ? You have all heard of the King of *Spain*'s Refignation ? Yes, R very well ' Why then, I'll let you fee a Piece of this Day's *Mercury* — From the *Amfterdam* Gazette, *February* 26th, N. ; Letters from *Madrid*, by the Way of *Paris*, advife, That notwithftanding the Refignation of the late King, the Miniftry ftill continue their Applications to him, on all important Occafions R. What do you think of that, Gentlemen ? C. 'Tis a very unaccount-able Bufinefs in Confcience ! R. You fee it is fo, tho' —— *H.* Upon my S— 'tis a ftrange Affair ! R. Nay further,— *Paris*, *March* 1ft, — The D. *de Bour-bon* has disbanded all the Troops kept in Pay by the

late

ļate D. of *Orleans,* and among thefe 1200 Colonels
broke —. There's a piece of News for ye —
Tb But what can be the Meaning of that ? *R.* 'swill,
Man, don't you fee it as plain as that Stoup is ftand-
ing before ye ? — (I' Gad that's certain —, take your
Drink. *R* Now, Gentlemen, I think, there's as much
News in thefe two Articles, as may fatisfy any reafon-
able Man about the prefent Pofture of Affairs But as
to the K. of *Spain's* Refignation, I'll tell ye a Story,
which perhaps none of ye has heard. Say on, Sir.
'Tis plain, that the young K. of *France* had got a Potion
from the late Regent, before the faid Regent died.
H Good Lord ! *R* Nay, hold. You know they can
make them up fo as to operate to any diftance of
Time they pleafe. *Tb* So they can, for I know a
Story —. *R.* Lord in Heaven ! Man, wilt thou
hear a Body fpeak. Now, Gentlemen, upon this the
King of *France* his Friends, gave the Regent a Potion that cut him off immediately. Say ye fo. *H.*
I vow to G - - -, I never knew that before. — *R.* Pati-
ence now ; The King of *Spain* finding this, and
knowing he could not fucceed to the Crown of

France

France, fo long as he held that of *Spain*, immediately ʳefigns in Favours of his Son. — *H.* God deliveᵣ ᵤs! And waits the Operation of the King of *France's* Potion — What can be plainer? *H.* By the - - - I knew it, — *Sir*, one wants ye. What's to pay Gentlemen? Nothing at all Sir, not a Farthing' Gentlemen, your moſt humble Servant.

S I R,

Yours, &c.

GEORGIO

GEORGIO DENUNO *Hadinenfi*,

JOANNES HARVAⒺUS,

De MORTE

GEORGII DAVIDSONI,

Illuftriffimi Comitis *Aboinii* Preceptoris fidelif-
fimi, qui ceffit Fatis *Id. Mar. Ann.* Partus
Viiginei MD CCXIX.

Ergo jacet fævis tandem pia victima fatis
    Nofter amor, noftrum, *Chare Denune*, decus ?
Cur tua mufa filet ? tantique in funere amici
Quid renuunt mœftos nunc tua plectra modos ?
An vatum Deus ipfe negat fub funere nati
Triftis opem ? triftes Aonidefque negant ?

        H   Ufque

Ufque licet renuant, propiiæ modulamine mufæ
Davididæ noftri fama peiennis erit

Fama perennis erit tiibuit quam Dia mathefis,
Cui ctaque quam fophiæ dogmata nota dabant.

Quam facilem fenfit Phœbum dum plectra movebat ?
Quam faciles doctas in fua vota Deas?

O decus! Aonii veneranda O gloiia cœtus
Davidide! patrii famaque l. ufque foli.

Te finceia files, te nefcia fallere dextra
Evehit ad fuperos, quos colis ufque, Deo.

Sic vixit, generofe, tuus pieceptor, *Alon?*,
Sic fuperat celfi flammea tecta poli

I decus, I noftrum, felicibus inclyte fatis,
Utere, & æterno carmina pange Dei.

Aftiæa fcandente polum fuiialibus aufis
Plena, tibi requiem barbara teria negat.

Aftræam Thæmidemque tuam, quas ufque colebas,
Ufque colas; animo numina grata tuo.

Relliquiis fuprema meæ pia vota camænæ,
(Quod folum potui) confecio, chare, tuis.

Ergo vale, nullis nomen non flebile mufis
Davidide! nofter luctus, amoique, vale.

E P I-

EPILOGUE

TO

Bellum Grammaticale.

Ladies' Perhaps, you guefs'd not our Intent,
So I come hear to tell ye what we meant,
As 'twere from *Beachy-head,* or from *La Hogue,*
I have return'd to fpeak the *Epilogue*

Then, to be fhort, we have been at the Wars,
But parted with whole Skins, we thank our Stars.
Two *Monarchs* fell together by the Ears,
And, Ladies, I muft own, I had my Fears,
A Poet and a Lover' Who wou'd thought it,
That they, of all Mankind, fhou'd e're have fought it?

In fhort, the Lovers haften to the Field,
And *Cupids,* Flames, and Hearts their Banners gild.

Vollies of parched Sighs inflame the Air,
Hope led the Vanguard, and the Rear *Despair*

Upon the ether Side, the Poet-Train
Their mighty Numbers pour upon the Plain
Squadrons of *Roundeliers* and *Rhymers* stand,
⁀ *Acrostics*, * *Anagrams*, a dreadful Band!
Two general *Charlo*'s at the Front appear,
And Quarter-Master *Doggrel* led the Rear.
Their Ensigns very old, but rowife nice,
All torn to Rags, embroider'd o'er with Lice.

But thank our Stars, just ere we drew our Swords,
(Choak'd as we were with Steams of Pannic T—s ;
We found the War was but a War of Words
Our *Poet-Monarch* chanc'd to be a *Noun*,
A Garret-gotten, hungry, loufy Lown ;
Guarded with *Adjectives*, as void of Senfe,
As, generally, the Poet is of Pence ,
With Pronouns, *He*'s and *She*'s, and *Who*'s and *Which*'s,
A fcoundrel Race of d—n'd pedantic B——s.

Again,

* *Metonym. Invent. pro Juv.*

Again, the *Lover-Prince* a Verb we found,
With Hopes and Fears completely guarded round;
Attended too by numerous Collections
Of *Adverbs, Prepositions, Interjections,*
As, *Utinam,* I wish— and, *Hei,* alace!
That e'er I saw that dear— deceitful Face.

But Ladies, Faith, if I stay longer here,
I'll turn upon the Lover's Side, I fear,
I see such pretty Faces all around me,
That ev'ry Glance, I'll swear, begins to wound me:
Farewel then, Ladies,— Gentlemen, *Adieu,*
Speak well of us, and we'll speak well of you;
Our Labour asks no other Recompence,
Commend our Wit, and we'll commend your Sense.

T O
The Much Honoured,
Sir RICHARD STEELE,
A POEM.

Qui feros cultus hominum
---- Formasti catus. Hor.

AS *Phebus* once, when banish'd by his Sire,
Touch'd on *Emathian* Plains the sounding Lyre,
The Satyrs, Nymphs, and all the Sylvan Train
Hung on each Note, and drunk the Heav'nly Strain'
Admetus wonders! And the Crowd around
Melts into Sense, and softens on the Sound ·
A milder Passion thrills thro' ev'ry Vein,
And Love and Music fill th' enchanted Plain.

Just

Juft fo, thy Precepts from each charming Page
Break on our Souls, and foften all our Rage.
Gods: How the fweet harmonious Pages fhine!
How the Thought brightens on each labour'd Line!
Before each Line a furly Paffion flies,
And a rude Thought on ev'ry Period dies.

Immortal *Steele!*

To thy dear Name, what Trophies can we raife,
How paint thy Merit in our Gothic Lays?
See! on *Edina's* Streets the Loving Throng
Gaze joyful as thou walk ft, and foftly wifh along
Our mingled Vows the Air, in Whifpers, bears,
And murmur'd Bleffings gently ftrike thine Ears.

All hail, thou gen'ious Friend! Thou haft been long
The Poets Darling, and their boafted Song.
A Northern Mufe, born near the freezing Sea,
Thaws into poor, but kindly Lays, for thee.
A Northern Mufe wou'd fondly borrow Fame,
Rife on thy Worth, and live upon thy Name.

But

But here, methinks, I fee thy Genius frown,
And fullen Lowrs the Ghoft of *Addifon*.

O *Addifon*! But ftop—The mighty Name
Rifes ftupendous! And looks down on Fame.
That Name, which fome have vainly ftrove to raife
On envious Merit, and detractive Praife;

Mean Artifice—

High on eternal Columns, fee, it ftands
Rear'd by his own, and *Steele*'s immortal Hands.

Adieu, Great *Steele*! Accept thofe humble Lays,
Shades of thy Worth, and Outlines of thy Praife;
If *Phœbus* fmiles upon a Northern Swain,
Perhaps his homely Mufe may 'ttempt a loftier Strain.

To Mr. C----

SIR,

I Don't know how to difpofe of this Evening, if you don't take a little of it off my Hands. 'Tis a very fine one, juft recover'd from a prodigious Rain. We'll drop the Scheme of Matrimony, if you pleafe, and try our Hand on fome Thing that won't ftick to us. I was laft Night invited by Mr. *W*---*p*, to go along with him to an Ale-houfe ; I own, a Bottle of Wine or two after Dinner, had pall'd my Appetite ; however, I had the Manners to comply. Away we went, and after a Bottle call'd for, and half empty, enters a Farmer or two, followed by an old Fellow of an inferiour, but independent Order. I'm as much for the Liberty of the Subject, as any Man, and indeed we found he had maintained his Privilege

I   pretty

pretty facredly, for the matter of a Century, or there abouts He told us in a Bumper or two, The Actions of *Montrofe* were a Jeft to him, and he cou'd tell Stor es a Quarter of a hundred Years older than the Dark *Munday*. I liftned very attentively to the venerable Author, and expected with Impatience, a Piece of ancient Entertainment, but a Farmer thrufting a Word or two a little violently in, the old Fellow turns refty, and gets the Difcourfe in his Hands over his Belly · He told us, with fome Emotion, that — but tock his Bon-per in the firft place — that he caw'd Quoals to my Lady Marquis of *Lothian*, and he was a Knave if ever he came hame that Day, without a Drink of the beft out of her Ladyfhip's awn Hands, and his Poutches as fow as they cou'd ftap, of as good Bread and Eeef, as ever a Quoalman fet his Teeth on· Na, Mr. *W----p*, an't pleafe your Honour; but God blefs the Family of *N---iie*, and here's to well mat they a' be, Rcot and Branch, an like your Honour, and God let me never die till I fee the Laird of *N---drie* upon his awn Town-Loan, as I ha' feen his Father before him, his Saul praife the Lord. I fay, an pleafe your Honour. However, I

met

met ae Afternoon with *David Meek*, I o'ertook him, Sir, at the Nook of the Dyke, as he came in to *Pepper-mill*, I fays, *Davy* Lad, what has tou gotten for the Quoals t'e Day? So he tells me, As I live to the L—, and ickwell I fanna make a Lye, C--- n C--- wi' my will, we drank, an like your Honour, a Night, aught and twinty Shilling the piece of Ale and Brandy, Bat what Divil car't I for that in thae Days, I was young Sir. — Here a Farmer interrupts, and tells us, he had brought home fome Reeds. For what End, fays Mr. W---p Says the old Fellow, For pointing the Thack, an't pleafe you, Sir, we bring them out of the Loch of *Diddingston*, an pleafe your Honour — Here's good Health and Happinefs to your Honour, and a' that belangs you. — O Lord, *Saners* G—, dinna ye mind fen we was pointing honeft Mr. G—*th*'s Houfe lang fine, O Man, fick Maun-fows of Peafe Cakes and Ale! O we had unco' Days o't, N----ry was a *N*---ry indeed then, and fine the great Pipe at Even, O' my S---, I danc'd my felf out of the Coot that Night, that was a forty Days Spring to me. God blefs the Houfe of *N*---ry, we had mony a merry Day under them, but I'm

turn'd

turn'd an ald Body now. God be wi' your Honour, thanks to your Honour for your Drink, God fens a' a fair End, an pleafe your Honour. — Farewell, *James. Exit.* — Says one of the Farmers, he's a good honeft raving Body ; Na, fays t'other, *Saners,* he's na fick a Fool as you take him to be — *Patrick,* I hinna fay the Man's a Fool, that's to fay, Man, a born Heado'wit. The Man has as muckle Wit as the Lord has been pleafed to len him, and the beft Man i'the Warld has na mair Na, *Saners,* I winna fay that nouther, but I ll fay, that *Jamie Brown* is not a born Hea lo'wit, I'll fay that. Lord, *Patrick,* I'm no f ·ing any Thing to the contrar, I fay, *Jamie Brown* has as muckle Wit as the Lord had gi'en him, and what wou'd you have mair, Man — That's true. — Put, be my Saul. — Dinna fwear by your Saul Man, 'tis no your awn. —— Well, Lord forgi' me Man, that's true —— But I'll fay this, for I ken what I'm faying - - - *Jamie Brown* is na that Fool that ye take him for. - - - Lord, *Patrick,* that's no the Thing that I'm faying. - - - Na, *Saners,* I'm no faying that, but I'll fay this, and I'll ftand to't. - - -

What

What fay ye, *Patrick*, I fay plainly, Deel be i'the Town that *Jamie Brown*'s beguil'd in. – – – God be wi' you, Lads. Farewell to your Honour. *Exit.* Mr. *W – – p,* and

Your humble Servant.

To Mr. M.

D Sir,

I'M forry to hear, by yours of the 20th, of your being fo extremely melancholy. You complain,
you are abandon'd to Wilds and Deferts, to Rocks and
Mountains, cover'd with eternal Snow; and that the
favage Inhabitants partake much of the Soil, and are
only fit Companions for their Neighbours of the Fo-
reft. I fhould be very fond of fome Methods to dif-
engage ye, and to reftore ye to your felf and to your
Friends. But fince you tell me, you're oblig'd to pafs
this Winter in this horrid Climate, I can only advife
ye to endeavour at finding out fome Amufement, in
order to beguile the Lonelinefs of the Place, as well
as the Severity of the Seafon. And I think really, the
beft Way is to turn Poet. That will keep your Head

warm

warm; and, generally speaking, those of your Country are not very apprehensive about the T—l.

I remember, I was once reduc'd to a State much like that of yours; I mean, to pass a Winter at a lonely Place, hard by an old ruinated Castle, that stood on the Banks of a pretty large Loch. I knew not in the World what to do with my self, during my Abode there: But happening to observe the above Castle inhabited by Owls and Ravens, and other Birds of Omen, I took a pretty odd Whim in my Head, and resolv'd to turn *Augur.* So at Nights, whenever I heard a Croak or a Whoo, I run always to the Door; and if I could but find out whereabouts the Head stood, I cou'd give a shrewd Guess at the Position of the A---, which is a considerable Step in the first Place In short, I advanc'd tolerably well in this Affair; so that, in a Month or two, I came to be taken Notice of, and employ'd by some honest Country People, concerning the Success of their Attempts, and what Days were properest to begin any considerable Enterprize upon, and so forth. I had pretty good Success truly, and my Divinations had gain'd

con-

confiderable Credit among the Vulgar When one
Night I happen'd to make my Obferves, as the Wind
blew from the Weft, the Head of my Bird of Pre-
fage directly fronting that Quarter; an honeft Wo-
man coming in, who had Occafion to go to a Market-
Town next Day, askt me, How I thought fhe fhou'd
fpeed, fhe having fome Butter and Cheefe along
with her to fell? I told her, The Butter wou'd do very
well; but for the Cheefe, I had little to fay to it. A-
gain, an honeft Man comes in, and asks me, How I
thought his Chickens and Eggs might go off next Mor-
ning? I had little Regard to the Chickens, but pronounc'd in Favour of the Eggs. In a word, Night
coming on, they return, and tell me, I had been extremely out in my Predictions , for Matters had
happen'd quite contrary to my Affertion The Cheefe
had gone clean off, but for the Butter --- The Chickens had a good Run, but not a Soul would meddle
with the Eggs. I was prodigioufly furpriz'd at this,
and could not imagine, how the Plague I had gone fo
damnably out of the Road I had prophefy'd like
other People before, and how this cou'd come about ---
At laft I remember'd, that the Night I made my Ob-
fervations,

fervations, the Wind had blown feverely from the Weft, which Way the Head of my boding Animal happened to ftand; and I, my felf, being directly Eaft from it, the Blaft had carried the Creature's Voice quite out of my Hypothefis, and made me predict upon a wrong Footing.

Upon this, the People began to fufpect my Skill, and to look upon me as little better than an Impoftor. However, the Seafon of the Year turning over, I had an Opportunity of leaving the Place, together with my precarious Art, and to return to the Society of a Set of Men, whofe Tafte was much above fuch Chimera's, and who knew not what it is to impofe, or to be impofed upon. I wifh your fpeedy Arrival amongft us, and am,

SIR,

Yours, &c.

K   De

D E

Georgii Buchanani Scoti,

Opeiibus,

Per Duos, *Tho. Ruddimannum & Ro. Fribar-num*, juris publici faciundis ;

Jo. Harvaeus.

MUſarum, *Buchanane*, decus' memorande tropæis
   Raptis Eois, Heſperiiſque plagis
Quas tulit aut Graia ,aut quas rettulit Itala tellus,
   Ad *Scotos* laurus, *Scote* beate, refers.
Non, tua mendacis Genevæ quod dogmata tingunt
   Scripta, tibi in doſto nunc datur orbe locus;
Carmina ſed clarium numen redolentia, cunſtos
   Et ſuperans Graios, Auſonioſque decus.

Nomine

Nomine & hoc folo, quod, ceu redivivus in orbem

    *(*Aufpice Friharno*)* denique prodis, erat.

Prodi igitur, non ante tamen, *Rudimanne,* fuprema

    Quam tua lima vetus fingat & ornet opus.

O *Buchanane* ! tibi quæ furget gloria, Phœbi

    Dum petis Eoas, Occiduafque domos ?

Quid dubitas auferre omnes quas Græcia laudes

    Afcræove feni, Mæoniove dabat ?

Et Maro concedet, molles qui & lufit amores,

    Jam fua Scotigenis carmina victa modis.

Vade igitur, cunctas donec penetraris ad oras,

    Scotorum & refonet nomen uterque polus.

EPILOGUE

TO A

PLAY

Acted at HADDINGTOUN.

DOwn from the Mother of all Womankind,
    The old crofs Rib, *ex traduce*, we find,
So that, you fee, — but further Demonftration,
A Female is a Shrew by Generation

  Nifa, you find, was as crofs-grain'd a Lafs,
As e'er that froward Virgin, old Queen Befs
When ought mifgave her, then fhe fat all furly,
Preluding to the Future *Hurly-Burly*,
Then in a Trice, a loud and fudden Rattle,
Gives the firft Signal to domeftick Battle.
Each Corner rings with Clamour, Brawl and Splutter,
And there poor Cully fits, and dares not mutter.

La-

Ladies, attend — and drop thefe dread Alarms,

Confult, if not your Eafe, at leaft your Charms.

Thefe Gufts of Paffion fudden Wrinkles bring,

And fhed fwift Autumn o'er your blooming Spring ;

When Maids, you may be nice, — but kind and gay,

Say no—but never think one Word you fay ;

Your Tongues and Eyes may wage eternal War,

Each Glance a Heav'n—And ev'ry Word—Defpair !

Still may the Tongue fay no—But for all this—

The kinder Eyes muft fpeak a charming—Yes!

So, Gallants, you this Leffon juft fhall find,

Women, by Contradiction, may be kind.

You by our Moral fee (which is not evil)

A loving Wife, made of a reigning Devil.

T ⊕

T O

Dr. *G. D.*

On his Tranflation of a Part of *Catullus*.

HAppy ! Thrice happy is the charming Maid,
  Who hath a Poet to her Toils betray'd ,
Obfcurely might fhe live, obfcurely dye,
Did not the Bard to her Affiftance fly ·
All that furvives her Urn, fhe owes his Flame,
Whofe deathlefs Numbers eterniz'd her Name.

This *Lesbia* in her fam'd *Veronian* found,
Nor more by him, than our foft Bard renown'd ;
By thee in fofter Notes fung on our Lawns,

Bright

Bright *Lesbia's* Praifes charm the wondring Fawns!

The Satyrs, Nymphs, and all the Sylvan Train

Trip, joyful, to thy Numbers o'er the Plain :

Forgetting Food, the Flocks in Silence gaze,

And, ravifh'd, liften to thy charming Lays.

How fmiles *Catullus* on th' Elyfian Plains,

To find his *Lesbia* live in *Britifh* Strains?

To find his Love-born Songs thus wafted o'er,

And warbl'd fofter on the *Britifh* Shore.

Fain wou'd I pay the mighty Debt I owe,

And bind the Bays on *Damon's* facred Brow;

Fain wou'd my Soul on foaring Pinions rife,

And waft his Fame, in Raptures, to the Skies :

But here the God forfakes my lab'ring Breaft,

And I can only pant —— and wifh the reft.

GEORGIO

✠✠✠✠✠✠✠✠✠✠✠✠✠✠✠✠✠✠✠✠✠✠✠✠✠✠✠✠✠✠✠✠
✠✠✠✠✠✠✠✠✠✠✠✠✠✠✠✠✠✠✠✠✠✠✠✠✠✠✠✠✠✠✠✠

GEORGIO DAVIDSONO

D E

POEMATE fuo ELEGIAGO

In obitum

ARCHIBALDI PITCARNII Scoti, M. D.

Jo. Harvaeus.

UT legi, ut ſtupui ! rurſus lectumque revolvo,
  Dignum Phœbea, *Docte,* poema lyra ;
Nec ſatiatus eram, miror nam numina Phoebi,
  Miror & inflatum tanto Helicone virum !
Digno digna viro tua carmina ; tu neque magnum
  Pitcarnum muſa lædis, amice, tua.

EIDEM,

✿✿✿✿✿✿✿✿✿✿✿✿✿✿✿✿✿✿✿✿✿✿✿✿✿✿✿✿✿✿✿✿
✿✿✿✿✿✿✿✿✿✿✿✿✿✿✿✿✿✿✿✿✿✿✿✿✿✿✿✿✿✿

E I D E M,

De P O E M A T E ad Dominum *D.*

R Ettulit Majæ mihi natus almæ
    Quod locis lætis animæ tuorum
Tippone in gyrum, babiofque rollos
                    Gnaviter urgent.

Sin ad illorum penetraffet aures
Fama, fe tantum genuiffe vatem,
Linquerent umbras, fuperas volentes
                    Tendere ad auras.

Tenderent, ut te clarioque gratum
Numini, ut te ter triplici choreæ
Cernerent, dignum meritoque te Par-
                  naffide lauro.

L   E P I-

EPILOGUE

TO A

PLAY

Aċted at HADDINGTOUN.

Ladies and Gentlemen,

OUR Play you've feen, and have approv'd our Wit,
 And I come here to thank the gen'rous Pit.
We've top'd our Parts, ai d you applaua our Rage;
And *Cato* fhines even on our youthful Stage.

But now I muft beg Leave to tell a Story,
And lay the Cafe, juft as it was, before ye,
Only becaufe the Scene was aċted heav'ly,
Allow me to be dull, and tell it gravely

In

In Eaftern Climes, a lofty Mountain ftands,
Which all the Southern *Scotifh* Coaft commands.
The higheft Heap of Beach I ever faw,
Our Country Swains call it *North-Berwick Law.*
Hard by this *Law* there ftands an antique Town,
Fam'd for its noble Patron's learned Gown,
For honeft Sauls, for Plenty and for Peace,
But more exceedingly for Solemn Geefe.
Thefe Geefe, amphibious now, we underftand,
Some breed by Sea, and others breed by Land.
The Land-Geefe are the queereft e'er were feen,
The other Day they mufter'd on the Green.
The Gander, who appears a jolly Bird,
Firft wav'd his Wings, and having dropt a T—d;
He thus began — Sirs, 'tis a pleafant Day,
What would you think, if we fhould act a Play?
The Flock confented, and they ftole our Farce,
But durft not 'ttemp our Play, fo they may kifs our A—
Ladies and Gallants, under due Correction,
I've told my Tale, you'll pardon the Reflection.

E S-

E S S A Y

In Imitation of the S P E C T A T O R,

Ingeni largitor venter. P E R S.

A S this is a Paper perfectly new and uncommon, and which I have been at a vaft deal of Pains to contrive a Name to, tho' without any vifible Succefs; fo I defign to treat it in a Way as odd as poffible, and fhall leave that of appropriating the Title, to my future Readers, if I fhall happen to have any.

But before I enter upon any other Subject, I beg Leave to obferve, that all Authors of whatever Kinds, or Complexions, Nations or Languages, have laid it down as an infallible firft Step into the World, either to prefix their Lives to their Works themfelves, or to have them prefixed by others; That is, if the Au-

thor

thor was a poor Fellow, he wrote his Life himfelf,
and took care to let the World know he was not a
Blockhead, however he might be a Beggar; and
told them plainly, that Folly and Poverty ought not
to be fo infeparably tacked together, as they common.
ly are : For, tho' an Author may be a poor Fel
low, yet he has Senfe in his Guts, and may writ as
well as a Blockhead of a thoufand a Year. On the o-
ther Hand, if the Author is a Man of Fortune, and
only writes for Pleafure, or for Reputation, why, he
hires a poor Dog to fet his Life in an advantageous
Light, in order to bribe the World over to his Lord-
fhip's or his Worfhip's Chara&ter, and his Writings. To
comply therefore, with this laudable Cuftom of my
Predeceffors, Contemporaries and Succeffors in the
Art of Scribling, I fhall let my Reader a little in
to my Life and Converfation, as far as is convenient
for my prefent Purpofe, and his Satisfa&tion.

In the firft place then, he muft know, I was born
in the Dominions of *Great Britain, France* and *Ire-
land*, juft about the Expulfion of the Defenders of
the Faith; and fo I have learnt from my Infancy

to

to live upon Hope ! 'Tis true, I have had but an airy Life on't, but have not been singular. When I was a young Fellow, about five or six, I remember, I had very surprising Notions of the King, and the Minister of the Parish , which Notions, as they were then but instinctive Idea's, I take them now to have been the dawning Impressions of that Regard I have since maintain'd for the Crown and the Mitre. About that Time, I had a natural Inclination to Pot_tage and Sowens ; but that the Reader may not fix my Nativity to the Sowen End of the Dominions, I must tell him, I had a tolerable Taste of a Pye or a Potato ; tho' to speak the Truth, my Genius gave most into a Bicker of Brose ! — So much for natural Appetites. Now, to my Acquisitions of Art; After I had made a tolerable Progress in the Bible, and was pretty well seen in the Acts of Sir *William Wallace*, my Father finding I had a competent Taste of blind *Hary*, *Glenkit* and *Gray Steel*, &c. in which Authors himself, honest Man, was really a great Master, and consequently a good Judge , and remembring likewise, when my Mother was big with me, she had dream'd she was brought to bed of a small Quantity of

Bays ;

Bays; he thought it high Time to fend me to the Grammar School. I went thro' its Exercifes, with all the Care and Application an abfolute Piece of bend Leather could infpire, and in due Time I arriv'd at the Univerfity. I forgot to inform the Reader, that by an Epitaph I wrote on a dead Cat, and a Piece of a Panegyrick on a Flefher Dog, while I was yet at School, my Father began to conceive pretty good Hopes anent my Mother's Dream. I arriv'd at laft' as I told you, at the Univerfity, where I got a tolerable fmattering of Creek, and fo entred upon the Logicks. I wrought till I was half mad at *univerfale a parte rei*, without being a jot the wifer, which gave me fuch a Difguft at that Art, or Practical Science, or what you pleafe to call it (for the Learned are not agreed there yet) that I could never endure to think of Logick fince. After I had gone thro' my Courfe, and had left the Univerfity, I can hardly tell what I did, for my Life has been fuch a Medley of Accidents and Incidents, &c. that I can give no diftinct Account of my felf. I fhall therefore conclude this Day's Work, tho' indeed I fhould have begun it with, an Account of my Name and Family.

My

My Name is *Nehemiah Numfcul,* of the ancient Family of the *Numfculs,* who, as I heard my Grandfir fay, pretended fome Affinity to King *Malcom Canmore;* For, added he, *Canmore* fignifying great Head, or great Scull, there's little or no Difference betwixt that and Numfcul; fo that they contend they are at leaft, a collateral Branch of that Prince's Family; Be that as it will, I can fay thus much for them, There is not a more ancient, or a more numerous Clan in the Dominions, nor a Tribe that has behaved themfelves more peaceably under all Governments, than the Race of the *Numfculs.*

ESSAY

E S S A Y

In Imitation of the

S P E C T A T O R.

THAT Tempeſt of Soul, which goes commonly under the Name of Paſſion, has been ſo nicely touched, ſo juſtly expoſed by every moral Author, in all Ages of the World, that a bare Catalogue of its Enemies were, I think, ſufficient, to frighten its Friends from their Alledgance, and bring them over to the ſerener Side · But after all, if a ſtormy Mortal finds himſelf Proof againſt his own Reflections, Names and Quotations will be to no Purpoſe in his Caſe; his Fire will have the better of his Reaſon, in ſpite of all the Diſcipline of the Porch · But, as this is not

M   what

what I defign to infift on, I have only introduc'd it as a Foil, to the Subject I fhall prefume to offer for your Entertainment.

Harmony, even before Matter had a Being, exifted from Eternity. It has no Dependence upon the Contrivances of Men or Angels, on Matter or Motion; its Duration is of an everlafting Date, nor is it any Thing but another Word for the Deity. The Creation, and all the different Species of Things there, reprefent Harmony only in *effigie*, as they are, but the Adumbrations, the faint Draughts and Out-lines of the Creator. Had it pleafed the Eternal, to have created a Race of Beings, with Faculties entirely oppofite to, and thwarting one another; Had he likewife been pleafed to have planted them in a World, whofe Motions run counter to every other moving Body about it, I fhall leave it to you to imagine the difmal State of thefe Animals, and to confider, what a dreadful Matter it were to be confin'd to the Society of fuch a wretched Set of Beings. But 'tis impoffible, by any Means, for GOD Almighty, to produce fuch a Piece of Creation. For, fince nothing can communicate to another,

another, what it has not in its felf; fo, it is impoffible for the Deity, who, as I hinted above, is the fame with Harmony, to produce Irregularity and Difcord. Which leads me to another, I think natural enough, Speculation. If Harmony is the Beauty, the Satisfaction, and the Life of every Being, if 'tis G O D himfelf, and the very Effence of Heaven, then certainly, Difcord is that, and that only, which we call *Hell*. It is not the Place, but the Inclinations of the Wicked, that make their *Hell*.

I fhall venture to add further, It is not G O D that damns Men, but Men damn themfelves: For, as I have faid, fince *Hell* is only the Effect of our vitious Faculties and Inclinations, as G O D Almighty could not create thofe Faculties, there was no Occafion for his creating or determining their Punifhment; becaufe, he knew it was a neceffary unavoidable Confequence of our Behaviour, fo that, it is not GOD that excludes us from the Place of Harmony and Blifs, but our felves, that cannot poffibly relifh or live in it.

This

This World, as I said, is but a faint Draught of the Deity, who is certainly the same with Harmony, and all the Beauties of the Creation, which we can possibly have any Taste or Notion of, must be nothing at all in Comparison of that ineffable Beauty and Harmony, that makes up the Creator But yet, how faint soever our Conceptions in that Case are, if we did but miss any Body we are acquainted with in the Solar System; nay, if there's but a disproportioned Feature in the most beautiful Face, If, on a flourishing green Tree, there shall be one withered Branch, I'll appeal to your Judgment, if it is not disagreeable. In a Word, every Thing (suppose it were but a Man with a disproportioned Staff in his Hand) choaks us, that is not downright Harmony and Concord

I shall only add, That Passion, or any irregular Heat or Emotion, is as certainly all we have here for *Hell*, as the little Harmony, we are capable of here, is our present earthly Heaven, and as we give into one or t'other, we get of Course a Habit of being *Happy*, or being *Miserable*, which shall improve and grow stronger by Degrees, and shall continue to be the inherent Faculty of our Souls to all Eternity.

I might have added, That the Harmony and Structure of the visible World, is entirely adapted to the Harmony and Structure of our Organs and Faculties, otherwise, it were impossible we could find any Pleasure in our present Situation, and likewise, as our Faculties improve, or to the better, or to the worse, so does our Happiness or Misery, as well in this, as in a future State.

F I N I S.

Lightning Source UK Ltd.
Milton Keynes UK
UKHW021952080519
342352UK00007B/180/P